Original title:
The Saltwater Dream

Copyright © 2025 Creative Arts Management OÜ
All rights reserved.

Author: Maya Livingston
ISBN HARDBACK: 978-1-80581-498-6
ISBN PAPERBACK: 978-1-80581-025-4
ISBN EBOOK: 978-1-80581-498-6

Lullaby of the Tide

The seagull sings a goofy tune,
As crabs dance round beneath the moon.
With jellyfish wearing hats so bright,
They twirl and spin, oh what a sight!

The echo of a wave's loud roar,
Calls fish to gossip on the shore.
They flail and flop in fits of cheer,
A splashy jig that we all hear!

Nautical Reveries

The fish all wear their finest scales,
They tell tall tales of daring gales.
With barnacles as best of friends,
They laugh and giggle 'til it ends.

A dolphin tries a juggling act,
With flying fish, a slippery pact.
Their splashy giggle fills the sea,
A comical sight, oh silly glee!

Hidden Currents

The octopus aims for a snack,
But trips on seaweed, oh what a hack!
With winks and blinks, he shakes his head,
While the starfish chuckles, 'Get well-fed!'

A clam would tell a story grand,
But only gurgles in the sand.
As bubbles float and tickle fins,
The ocean's laughter never ends!

Dunes of Desire

At sunset, sandcastles reach for stars,
With buckets full of snacks and jars.
A crab sits down to eat his cake,
But finds his treat is now a fake!

The sandy shores are filled with cheer,
As gulls drop fries from just up near.
We laugh and shout, oh joyful screams,
In this wild place of sunny dreams!

Saltwater Sonnet

Crabs in tuxedos dance on the shore,
While seagulls gossip, never a bore.
A beach ball flies, with a loud, silly cheer,
Making all the kids jump into the clear.

Flip-flops flop as they race to the tide,
Chasing the waves that giggle and slide.
Fishermen caught in a hilarious mess,
As fish steal their bait, what a funny guess!

Breath of the Sea

Waves whisper secrets, tickling the sand,
Shells wearing hats, so fashionable and grand.
The ocean splashes with a wink and a grin,
While dolphins jump high, they're ready to spin.

With salty hair, we dance in the breeze,
As crabs do the cha-cha with such silly ease.
Laughter erupts like a bubbly sea foam,
This seaside party feels just like home!

High Tide Hopes

At high tide, surfboards take a sweet leap,
A dog on a floaty, not missing a beat.
Sandcastles crumble, oh what a surprise,
As seagulls circle with mischievous eyes.

Splashing through puddles, we giggle and wriggle,
As octopuses wave with a wiggly jiggle.
The sun drinks our sunscreen, oh what a sight,
We're all just goofballs, under the light!

Oceanic Embrace

The tide rolls in with a comical sneeze,
As beach towels flop like a runaway breeze.
Goggles on faces, laughter in the air,
Balloon animals float, wandering without care.

The jellyfish jiggle, oh what a delight,
As kids chase their shadows, running so bright.
Salty snacks disappear, giggles abound,
With every splash, new friendships are found.

Seaglass Reveries

Once a sharp bottle, now smooth and green,
The ocean's a magician—what a scene!
Buried treasure in sand, it twinkles with glee,
A lopsided youth, now wise as can be.

Old shoes washed ashore, still searching for feet,
They chuckle and gossip, oh what a feat!
With every wave's whisper, tales drift and glide,
Making us giggle at life's silly ride.

Dance of the Ocean

The jellyfish waltzes, a graceful ballet,
While crabs cut a rug, then scamper away.
Seagulls are DJing on seashells so bright,
Dropping beats with the splashes, what a delight!

Waves do a cha-cha, it's quite the display,
The fish join the conga, no need for ballet.
Each splash is a joke that the tide loves to tell,
In this hopping seaside, we all dance so well.

Tempest and Tranquility

The wind howls like laughter, a wild, funny spree,
While waves throw confetti, as if to agree.
A storm wears a cape, like a clumsy old clown,
And sunshine peeks out, wearing bright, silly crowns.

Raindrops do ballet on umbrellas we hold,
As tempests tickle, it's a sight to behold.
But peace is a jester, quiet yet sly,
Playing pranks in the calm that makes hearts fly high.

Shoreline Reflections

Footprints parade, a quirky march line,
As crabs steal the show, performing divine.
Each step in the sand wears a grin from the sun,
In this wavy circus, life's all about fun.

Mirrors of the sea laugh back at your face,
Making waves of mischief, such a playful place.
With laughter and splashes, let worries just flee,
In this sandy wonderland, just let it be free.

Voyage of the Heart

Set sail on a leaf, what a strange trip,
With jellyfish dancing a whimsical flip.
The seagulls giggle, cracking a joke,
While the fish in the sea play a game of folk.

My compass is lost, spinning around,
Chasing a crab that scuttles aground.
The waves give a cheer, what a zany ride,
As I float on a dream, with laughter as my guide.

Mosaic of the Sea

Painted with colors, the ocean does glow,
With starfish in bow ties, putting on a show.
A whale tells a tale, quite absurd and wild,
While turtles roll by, grinning, beguiled.

Coral reefs giggle with shades of the bright,
Dancing to rhythms of waves in delight.
A pelican drools with the catch of the day,
As sea beans are tossed in a comical play.

Footprints of the Sailor

A sailor once said, 'My boots are too big!'
As he tripped on a wave, did a flip and a jig.
The sand made a mark, an outline so neat,
Of a very confused man with wobbly feet.

With a wink at a clam, he shared some old tales,
Of mermaids with legends and gossiping gales.
His laughter echoes in the serene bay,
As he prances away, what a sight, hip-hip-hooray!

Beneath the Marine Veil

Bubbles rise up, a party in place,
With octopi dancing in a dizzying race.
A conch shell's a mic, for the gossipy shrimp,
Sharing secrets of fish, grumpy and prim.

Anemones sway, just tickling the sea,
While plankton sing tunes, so light and so free.
Beneath swirling currents and bubbles so fine,
We laugh with the ocean, oh what a divine!

Whispers of Ocean Tides

Seagulls squawk with glee,
While crabs dance on the sand.
A starfish flipped and free,
Waves tickle their tiny hands.

Bubbles float like balloons,
Fish are laughing with delight.
The ocean hums soft tunes,
As dolphins pull off tricks so tight.

Shells giggle at the shore,
While seaweed waves hello.
A jellyfish wants to score,
But forgot its dance, oh no!

Tides roll in with a cheer,
Sandcastles feel quite grand.
Yet a wave crashed most near,
And left a splashy brand.

A Journey Beneath Waves

Octopus wearing a hat,
Says, 'Join my parade, my friend!'
Squid twirl and do acrobat,
While sea turtles laugh and blend.

A whale sings a tune out loud,
His voice echoes through the sea.
Fish gather, they form a crowd,
Dancing in such harmony.

Anemones wave and wink,
'Join us for a jelly feast!'
But beware, don't take a drink,
Or you may just become a beast!

Sunlight sparkles like a dream,
Through coral lanes we twirl and play.
Bubbles pop—we squeak and beam,
Underwater, we dance all day.

The Lure of Salty Breezes

Seagulls steal a sandwich slice,
While I'm busy with my fries.
Salty breezes feel so nice,
But I'll keep my food—no lies!

The beach ball flies with flair,
Only to land in a wave.
Laughing mermaids toss in air,
Dreams of a beachball rave!

Flip-flops slap, a child screams,
As the tide pulls back with a roar.
My ice cream drips, or so it seems,
Melt like thoughts—oh, what a chore!

Breezes bring a funny chill,
As I race to catch my hat.
But the wind has stronger will,
Than the best of feline acrobats!

Reflections on a Shimmering Surface

Mirror-like, the water shines,
A fish jumps to take a look.
With a splash, it breaks the lines,
Then whispers, 'Hey, come read a book!'

A crab reads with tiny claws,
While sea cucumbers recline.
'This story gives me pause!'
'What's that? A wave? Oops, it's mine!'

The sun dips down with a grin,
Sea stars cheer as night draws near.
They plan a beach ball spin,
But fall over in a cheer!

Reflections gleam, but so do we,
Waves are winking, what a sight!
And laughter floats in jubilee,
As we dance away the night.

Tidepool Reverie

Tiny crabs in a race,
Who'll be first to claim the space?
Starfish lounging, quite the scene,
In this pool where they convene.

Glimmers sparkling, oh what fun,
Where water tricks under the sun.
Anemones waving hello,
As goofy fish put on a show.

Seashells gossip, whispering tales,
Of seaweed waves and silly gales.
Every tide brings a new charade,
In this wavy masquerade!

So let's splash in, no time for gloom,
Nature's our stage, a lively room.
With laughter echoing in each wave,
We're enjoying life, oh how we rave!

Embrace of the Celestial Sea

Stars above in a glittery race,
While jellyfish drift with a silly grace.
A whale's joke, do they have a pun?
Just ask the fish, they'll say it's fun!

Octopus juggling with all eight hands,
Clams keep wishing for better bands.
Sea turtles slow dance, no rush at all,
Their moves are grand, but they're prone to fall.

Shells are the gossip, catching the trend,
Who wore it best, is it seashells or friends?
Crabs play charades, acting quite sly,
Their poker face is a comical lie!

So celebrate waves under the night,
With bubbles popping, a pure delight.
Swim in the joy, no troubles in sight,
In this watery world, life's all about delight!

Echoes of Distant Shores

Waves where seagulls make a fuss,
"Is that a crab? Or just a bus?"
Sandcastles leaning with a wink,
"Watch me fall! I promise, I stink!"

Seashells chatting, passing the news,
Of sunken treasures and silly blues.
Turtles wearing shades, oh so cool,
Teaching fish the art of being a fool.

In the foam, a treasure hunt begins,
Finding lost socks, perhaps other sins.
Laughing at waves that trip and fall,
The ocean's comedy, a spectacle for all!

So grab a float, let's ride the spree,
With cooler laughter, you and me.
The shore breaks giggles, let's not ignore,
This is life's ocean, forever to explore!

Dancing with Dolphins

Dolphins twist in the sparkling spray,
Making loops that brighten our day.
With giggles echoing through the blue,
"Catch us if you can, we're fast, it's true!"

Whales sing tunes that hum like bees,
While schools of fish dance with ease.
"In this party, you've gotta shake!"
Even sea urchins join for fun's sake!

Barnacles boast of their old-time fame,
"I stuck around, can you say the same?"
Each bubble bursts with a funny sound,
As friends dive in, merriment abound.

So let's twirl under the sun's bright gaze,
With splashes and laughter, we'll set the stage.
Dance with the sea, let your spirit soar,
In this watery realm, laughter's the core!

Currents of Introspection

In a jellyfish suit, I take a leap,
My thoughts swim deep, like a fishy creep.
With each wave's laugh, my worries drip,
Sea turtles giggle, they give me a tip.

Waves frolic around, they tease and shout,
My floaty gets stuck; I whirl about.
A dolphin grins, showing teeth so white,
Still not as bright as my swim trunks tonight.

Sandcastles wobble in quirky shapes,
Seagulls dance, plotting their pranks and drapes.
Shells talk back, sharing their own tales,
Of crabby characters and their epic fails.

In foam and spray, my fears drift away,
I dive for the sun and frolic all day.
With laughter and splashes, it's quite the scene,
In this silly paradise, life's a funny routine.

Between the Waves

Lobsters are gossiping over a brew,
While starfish get tipsy on salty skew.
A crab plays cards with an octopus dear,
With eight hands in play, it's hardly unclear.

Barnacles dance on a boat made of cheese,
While seagulls complain of the briny breeze.
My beach ball's a pirate, it rolls away fast,
Chasing it down, oh what a stinky blast!

Mermaids with ukuleles serenade,
I try to join in but my voice starts to fade.
The tide laughs loudly, it's quite the finesse,
Turns out my singing's a nautical mess.

But giggles abound, and it's never a bore,
As waves toss my thoughts onto sandy shore.
Between all the splashes and sunny delight,
My worries dissolve; everything feels right.

Seaside Secrets

The tide whispers tales in a breathy hush,
Beneath my flip-flops, I feel the rush.
Clams offer gossip, they're quite the chat,
While seaweed winks, playing peekaboo brat.

I find a lost sock that swam far and wide,
It's now a sea legend, with fish as its guide.
The crabs throw a party for ocean debris,
Wearing old bottles, they're fancy as peas!

Dolphins do flips with a mischievous flair,
While I try to dive but just splash everywhere.
They say, "Join the fun! Learn to surf on a wave!"
I send in my floaty, that brave little knave.

With laughter and bubbles, secrets are spun,
As gulls overhead join in on the fun.
In a quirky seaside, we share tales anew,
As laughter floats high, like the sky's sunny hue.

Nautical Nightfall

Stars twinkle bright as the sea starts to hum,
A whale sings low, while the jellybeans drum.
With moonlit vibes, I spot a sweet crab,
He dances on rocks, what a curious fab!

The anchor's lost, and so is my shoe,
The ships in the harbor are joining the view.
Rats on a rigging share cheese on a board,
And laughter erupts, it feels so adored.

Mariners chuckle at the fishes' plight,
While clam shells gossip about last night's fright.
Tides roll in secrets, both silly and deep,
As I join the chorus, I can hardly keep.

The night holds its breath, as I take a stand,
With all of my pals, we make quite the band.
In this whimsical world where the sea meets the sky,
Life's a wobbly dance, oh me, oh my!

Mariner's Longing

A pirate's hat up on my head,
I think my crew has gone to bed.
The sea's my friend, but it won't pay,
For all the fish I lost today.

I waved goodbye to my last catch,
It swam away with quite a scratch.
The seagulls laugh, they steal my fries,
They're plotting from their salty skies.

A mermaid winked, I dropped my oar,
And nearly fell right off the shore.
With every wave, they tease and leap,
While I just dream of roasted sheep.

So here I am, on deck I sway,
Trying to find my sense of play.
With jellyfish as company,
Each wave, a giggle, wild and free.

Where the Sea Meets Sky

The ocean's blue, the sky's in pink,
I saw a shark that made me think.
It grinned so wide, I thought it smiled,
But lunch for it was quite beguiled.

The gulls do squawk, they hoot and holler,
As I dive for the last sea dollar.
I slip and slide on fishy scale,
Then chase my boat as it sets sail.

A dolphin jumps, it steals my hat,
I chase it down, imagine that!
"Bring back my cap!" I start to shout,
It rolls its eyes, then flips about.

With waves of laughter in the breeze,
I build a sandcastle with such ease.
Where sea meets sky, it's pure delight,
A comic ballet in the twilight.

Lost in the Swell

I drifted far, oh what a ride,
A rubber ducky by my side.
The waves they danced, I lost my shoe,
Now it's a quest, with no real clue.

Posh crabs watch with judgmental stares,
As I tumble 'round without a care.
A buoy floats past, I wave it down,
"Hey buddy, can you turn this 'frown'?"

In the swirl of frothy cheer,
I might take a nap, or grab a beer.
With salty snacks and giggles galore,
I'm lost at sea, but I want more!

So here I flail, a carefree jest,
Floating 'round in my sea-bound quest.
Where every splash is laughter made,
In a world where troubles just fade.

Beneath the Briny Surface

What's lurking down beneath the waves?
An octopus with super knaves?
With playful tricks it shows its flair,
I think it winked; I almost stare.

I burbled with a fishy grin,
While pelicans flew overhead, thin.
They squawked and swooped, with hooks in beak,
I clutched my snacks as I turned meek.

A crab approached, it asked, "What's new?"
I said, "Just floating, how about you?"
We shared some tales of salty spice,
While dodging jellybeans—precise!

Beneath the briny bits I roam,
In a goofy, swaying fishy home.
Each bubble burst, a giggle might,
As I explore this wacky sight.

Call of the Deep

Bubbles rise to greet the sun,
A fish in shades of purple fun.
He swam the length of a disco ball,
Said, "Best dance floor? The ocean's all!"

Turtles wearing tiny hats,
Debating who is king of chats.
The jellyfish threw a glowing rave,
While starfish just tried to misbehave!

An octopus with eight left feet,
Keeps tripping over seaweed neat.
A crab with shades looked quite absurd,
Reciting poetry, quite unheard.

So if you find a fish that sings,
Examine closely what it brings.
Underwater giggles fill the air,
In salty seas where dreams don't care!

Scattered Seashells

On a shore where laughter roams,
Seashells tell their secret homes.
A conch blew tunes of lost delight,
While clams just grumbled, feeling slight.

A sand dollar pranced with glee,
Claimed to be royalty of the sea.
A sea urchin tried to join the crew,
Their prickly charms just wouldn't do.

A starfish posed for selfies bright,
While dolphins danced in sheer delight.
Anemones waved as if to cheer,
Inviting all to join the sphere!

With every wave, a tale unfolds,
Of quirky finds and treasures bold.
Laughter echoes, buoyant and free,
In the scatter of shells by the sea!

Reveries of Fishermen

Fishermen with nets so wide,
Dream of catches, none to hide.
First one claimed a whale's embrace,
But it stole his lunch with grace!

With rods and reels, they tell their tales,
Of great escapes and slippery fails.
One lost a shoe in monster's jaws,
And learned to fish without his paws!

Their boats, a-fluttering by the shore,
Sometimes drift off—never more!
As gulls giggle, taking their bait,
"Mackerel?" they ask, "Or just your fate?"

But amidst this madness, they unite,
In laughter shared beneath the light.
For fishing's more than just a catch,
It's stories spun with every scratch!

Resonance of the Abyss

In the depths where sunlight fades,
Creatures play pranks in dark charades.
A ghostly fish pretended to scare,
While others just twinkled without a care.

A whale sang opera, quite offbeat,
Echoes bounced like wild retreat.
Sardines formed a marching band,
As krill danced through bubbles unplanned.

An anglerfish flicked its light,
Trying to attract a fancy sight.
But all it snagged was a lost shoe,
And a crab that completely flew!

Down in the deep where humor flows,
Even the trenches wear fin-approved clothes.
With laughter riding each salty wave,
In shadows where mischief misbehaves!

Beyond the Lighthouse

Seagull overhead, making quite a show,
Shouting loud secrets that nobody knows.
A crab in a hat, he's strutting in style,
Snapping his claws with a cheeky smile.

A fish in a bowtie, he's ready to dance,
Twisting and wriggling, he takes a chance.
Waves are his partners, they swirl and they sway,
To a tune that only the ocean can play.

Fragments of the Seascape

The octopus juggles with shells and a shoe,
While dolphins are giggling, a merry crew.
A starfish is sunbathing, cheeky and bold,
Telling tall tales that never get old.

A pirate's pet parrot is singing off-key,
Squawking of treasures and endless sea.
The waves clap their hands as if they agree,
This underwater circus is wild and free.

Drifted Dreams

A rubber duck floating, all blissful and bright,
Claims to be captain, ruling the night.
With a wink and a quack, it conquers the foam,
Inviting sea turtles to join in its dome.

Beach balls go bouncing, in love with the breeze,
Chasing down memories, with such joyful ease.
Shells whisper stories, half-spoken, half-dreamed,
In a world where nothing is quite as it seemed.

Harmonies of the Ocean

A clam with a ukulele, playing so sweet,
Sings of adventures, a real tasty treat.
Anemones sway to the rhythm of fun,
Earning their stripes as the day's number one.

Turtles in sunglasses, cruising with flair,
Making a splash in the salty sea air.
They laugh at the waves that come in for a nudge,
Proclaiming, 'This ocean is our favorite judge!'

Distant Shores

On sandy banks, the seagulls trot,
They steal my fries without a thought.
The waves, they giggle in sea foam lace,
While crabs dance funny, keeping pace.

With flip-flops flying, I make a splash,
A wave's embrace, oh! What a crash!
The sun so bright, it makes me squint,
And dolphins leap as if to hint.

A treasure hunt for bits of shell,
I trip and fall, but all is well.
A starfish winks, it's quite a sight,
As seabirds swoop, oh what a flight!

But in this shore-bound comedy,
My laughter rings in harmony.
With stories told of sea-bound lore,
The distant shores keep me wanting more.

Visions Beneath the Surface

Beneath the waves, where fishes grin,
I try to swim but just fall in.
With goggles on, I spot a clown,
Who juggles bubbles, wearing a crown.

A jellyfish, it floats on by,
I think it winked, or maybe I lie.
A turtle spins a tales of yore,
While all the seaweed laughs on the shore.

An octopus waves its arms with glee,
It tickles my toes, oh, what a spree!
A sea cucumber rolls on its back,
I giggle hard, the ocean's knack.

It's a splashy show in blue and green,
With antics that are rarely seen.
From coral castles to sandy beds,
The visions here spin fun in threads.

Songs of Anemones

In the garden of sea, the anemone sways,
With colors bright that dance all day.
A fish with stripes in goofy lines,
Rides the currents like roller coasters' vines.

Swaying along to a bubbly tune,
They throw a party beneath a moon.
With sea snails wearing hats of green,
The craziest critters you've ever seen!

A shrimp breakdances on a coral stage,
While a clam just hides, quite in a rage.
They sing of sushi, they sing of fun,
In this watery world, I'm number one.

As bubbles rise, laughter flows,
Each note a wave that gently grows.
Songs of joy, a playful theme,
With anemones swaying in the dream.

Castaways in the Current

We float adrift, on this rubber raft,
With snacks stored well, in case we draft.
A fish named Phil gives us a grin,
As seagulls swoop down to steal my tin.

We paddle hard but go in loops,
While dolphins giggle, teasing groups.
The tide pulls us, Lord knows where,
With sea monsters playing truth or dare.

A message in a bottle we find in jest,
Turns out it's just a sailor's quest.
With sun hats tilted askew on heads,
We laugh as waves make silly beds.

So here we are, castaways alone,
With salty winds and dreams well-known.
Adventure calls from currents wide,
We float along, our joy our guide.

A Voyage to Solitude

I set sail with a sandwich and a smile,
Waves tickling my toes, oh what a style!
The seagulls caw, calling me a clown,
While I contemplate sailing with my pants down.

Fish giggle as they swim by with grace,
Catching my line, but fleeing the chase.
My boat's made of dreams, or maybe just wood,
With every wrong turn, I'm lost in the flood.

Carried by the Aquatic Winds

Wind whispers secrets, giggles in the breeze,
It blew off my cap, oh, if only it sees!
I chase after flotsam, like it's a parade,
Only to find I'm lost in charades.

My compass spins wildly, what's north? What's south?
Do I follow my heart or the seagull's mouth?
Each gust brings a chuckle, a tickle of fun,
In this silly adventure, I'm the only one.

Enchanted by the Horizon's Glow

The sunset dances, colors twist and twirl,
A hotdog in hand, oh, watch it unfurl!
I wave to a dolphin, who seems quite bemused,
As my mustard's escaping, totally confused.

Shimmering waters, where jellyfish glide,
I might join them, or at least take a ride.
With laughter and snacks, I befriend a crab,
Together we cackle, what a silly fab!

Secrets Drifted on the Waves

Secrets float by on a bubble of foam,
Whispers of fish who turn water to home.
They gossip of currents, of mermaids at play,
While I scout for treasure from yesterday's bay.

My bucket's half full, but so is the tide,
What's in here, a shell or a fish that has lied?
With jokes in the waves, I'm swept off my feet,
In this whimsical ride, laughter's the treat!

Sunlit Depths

In waters bright, a fish called Fred,
Wore a tiny hat upon his head.
He danced with grace, all quite absurd,
While seahorses giggled, how they heard!

A crab named Larry joined the show,
With pinchers clapping, stealing the glow.
A dolphin's laugh rang through the sea,
As jellyfish swayed, wild and free.

They all agreed on one fine goal,
To paint the reef a bright, bold soul.
With bubbles rising, brushes in fin,
They glittered the ocean, let the fun begin!

So if you dive where the sunrays play,
Join in the antics, swim and sway.
For laughter echoes through every wave,
In watery depths where the silly behave!

Nautical Daydreams

A sailor's hat on a whale named Clyde,
Glided through currents, full of pride.
With a wink to the gulls, he'd spin around,
Creating splashes, laughter abound.

A parrot squawked, wore shades of blue,
"Yo ho!" he chortled, "What's your next view?"
They plotted treasure not made of gold,
But sandwiches, pickles, all quite bold.

The octopus served fishy delights,
While sea turtles danced under moonlit nights.
Bubbles burst forth, a joyful spree,
In nautical dreams, all silly and free.

So join the crew, under skies so vast,
Where goofy giggles and joy hold fast.
In every wave, in every beam,
Sail on, my friend, in a daydream!

The Rhythm of the Reef

In a coral town where the seaweed sways,
    A band of fish began to play.
  Tuna on drums, with fins so fine,
While starfish clapped, "Isn't this divine?"

A clownfish joked, donned a wig of kelp,
Swirling through rhythms, oh what a kelp!
  The sea anemones swayed to the beat,
    As dolphins flipped in a dance so neat.

"I can't believe this underwater jam!"
  Said a turtle slow, with a quirky slam.
  From foamy bubbles to sandy floors,
    Laughter echoed from ocean doors.

So join the dance, feel the ocean's cheer,
    For in the reef, no worries near.
  With every beat, hazy and bright,
The rhythm will carry you into the night!

Salty Kisses

A mermaid with shells in her hair,
Did a twirl, with sea crabs in despair.
"Stop pinching, you little flirts!" she sighed,
As waves rolled over, and laughter dried.

A clam popped open, a secret to share,
"Best shower and sunning, beyond compare!"
The fish all giggled, with scales agleam,
In salty mist, they lived the dream.

They sipped on sea foam, from cups of sand,
Playing tag with a blowfish band.
The octopus winked, with all eight arms,
Having fun with their silly charms.

So roam the shore, let laughter abound,
With salty kisses where joy is found.
In this frothy world, with breezy cheer,
Dance through the tides, with friends so dear!

Woven from Waves

A jellyfish danced, oh so spry,
It twirled like it knew how to fly.
I asked it to teach me the moves,
It wobbled away, the joker proves.

The crabs held a meeting, in tiny suits,
They argued over the best of fruits.
One claimed it was the kelp snack feast,
But everyone know, they preferred the yeast!

The fish threw a party, scales shining bright,
They glittered like stars in the soft moonlight.
With bubbles of laughter and winks from the sea,
They laughed till the tide pulled away with glee.

The seashells collected, for they have no shame,
Rumors of beachcombers, their only fame.
With secrets whispered, they build quite a scene,
In the world of the waves, they're the reigning queen!

Tidal Dreams

At dawn, the waves laugh, a giggly affair,
Seagulls play tag, flying high in the air.
A sandcastle fell, the tide couldn't wait,
"Sorry, my friend, you were just second rate!"

The starfish suggested they hold a parade,
But the octopus said, "I won't be dismayed.
I'll wear all my hats, I'm a fashionable sort!"
Then the sea cucumbers rolled in for sport.

The dolphins cracked jokes, they flipped to amaze,
With their comedic flair, they'd steal the day's praise.
They invited the squids to join in with laughter,
And soon the ocean was a stage for disaster!

As night falls, they toast with seaweed delight,
The deep water cream soda's just right.
With bubbles and giggles, they drift into dreams,
In the ocean's embrace, it seems silly, it gleams!

Deep Blue Visions

A whale with a hat and a monocle rare,
Swam past a schoolfish in need of a pair.
"Good day!" he exclaimed, "Care to join in my quest?"
But the schoolfish just giggled, "You're truly the best!"

In the coral club, they held quite the ball,
Where the clams shimmied while the snails had a brawl.
The shrimp served the drinks, it was wild and bizarre,
Even the anemones sang from afar!

The sea turtles winked, sported shades made of glass,
While the pufferfish puffed, an impressive mass.
They cheered for the squid, their dance was a hit,
With spins and with swirls, he danced with great wit.

As the tides rolled in, the night brought a cheer,
With laughter and joy, they held each other dear.
In the deep blue, the dreams swirled and swayed,
In a whirlpool of fun, youthfulness displayed!

Under the Sail

A pirate crab with a parrot on deck,
Shouted "Yo-ho-ho" with a raucous peck.
His ship made of shells, sailed lightly ashore,
But tripped on a starfish, oh what a score!

The dolphins took bets on how far he'd glide,
While the seagulls just cawed from the sky, full of pride.
"Will he rescue the treasure or perhaps just a snack?"
With waves of laughter, they cheered on the crack.

There, mermaids sang songs of the zany old days,
Of mishaps and blunders in marvelous ways.
With long flowing hair and glittery tails,
They spun through the water while telling tall tales.

Under bright sails, the fun never stopped,
With friends on the sea, laughter always topped.
In this merry whirl, the world felt so right,
The ocean's embrace brought joy through the night!

Siren's Call

Upon the shore I heard a song,
A mermaid's voice where I belong.
She promised gold, a fishy fate,
But all I found was a crab on my plate.

She danced around, with fins a-flash,
While I just tripped and made a splash.
"Come swim with me!" she giggled loud,
I waved goodbye, my head in a cloud.

Her seaweed hair, like tangled thread,
I thought of those who might be misled.
Someday, she'd need a stylist's hand,
But I'm no expert on ocean brand.

I left her there with a flip and a twist,
Couldn't quite charm what I'd missed.
Dry land awaits with another snack,
Forget the deep; I'll take my flack.

Waves of Wandering

The tide pulled in, like pizza dough,
And I, the toppings, washed to and fro.
Each wave a joke, a splashy jest,
Where do you go? I'd like to rest!

I built a castle made of sand,
But waves conspired, oh so grand!
With every wall, a playful tease,
"Here comes the tide!" It brings me to knees.

A seagull laughed from high above,
I swear it knew I did not shove!
With ice cream cone and salty breeze,
Life's a joke that never leaves.

So here I sit, with grains in my flip,
A salty soul on a silly trip.
Each wave a tale, each laugh a dream,
The ocean's art, a quirky theme.

Wind and Water

The wind was raucous, quite a hoot,
Blew off my hat and chased my boot.
"Catch me!" it whispered with a grin,
While I just chuckled at my win.

The waves they danced like lively sprites,
While I fell over, oh what sights!
"You can't take me!" I called out loud,
But they just laughed, as if they're proud.

I mulled my fate, my klutzy charm,
With sopping shoes, but none the harm.
The tide came in, my pants were soaked,
Yet in this chaos, laughter provoked.

Hold tight, I thought, my wiggly dreams,
Life's a circus, or so it seems.
As wind and water share a laugh,
I ride this wave, my silly path.

Resilient Reflections

In puddles splashed, my face appeared,
A tableau of fear, but laugh I steered.
With salty curls and playful frown,
I gazed below, a jester's crown.

The ocean's mirror showed me strange,
A dancing fool, oh the range!
"Embrace the wave, take on the tide!"
With a tiny boat, I would not hide.

Each ripple laughed, a cheeky tease,
And I, the clown, laughed with ease.
I tried to swim, but oh dear me,
A fish just winked; it's not so easy!

So here I float, both silly and proud,
The water whispers, laughter loud.
A swirl of joy, a twist of fate,
In life's odd pool, I celebrate!

An Ode to the Forgotten Cove

In a cove where seagulls sing,
A crab once tried to do the swing.
He slipped on sand, oh what a sight,
Wobbled off in pure delight.

The tide rolled in like a big ol' friend,
And knocked the crab into a bend.
His dance became a splashy show,
As fish laughed on in the undertow.

Sunbathers tumbled with their snacks,
While dodging waves, they'd bust their backs.
The sunbeam slipped with a slippery grin,
As laughter echoed, thick and thin.

So here's a toast to waves that sway,
And crabs who dance with a little play.
The forgotten cove, a joyful place,
Where fun collides with the ocean's grace.

Beyond the Reach of the Shore

Beyond the waves where surfboards glide,
A sea turtle took a bathroom ride.
With a splash and a flipper flail,
He headed off on a wild, wet trail.

A fisherman caught nothing but air,
While dolphins giggled, unaware.
They pulled pranks with a flip of a tail,
Creating tales that would set sail.

Sandcastles built with nice, big dreams,
Were flattened fast by tidal teams.
Children cried as their castles fell,
Yet laughed again, what a swell spell!

So frolic on, dear wave and foam,
In this funny, coastal home.
Where moments live, wild and bright,
Beneath the sun, in warm delight.

Unfolding the Sea's Stories

Oh, the tales the ocean knows,
Of silly fish in wiggle shows.
They wear the seaweed like a crown,
While jellyfish dance without a frown.

The octopus tried to tie his shoe,
But each leg danced to a different cue.
He wriggled, jiggled, round and round,
Till he simply fell flat on the ground.

Seashells whisper secrets loud,
Of crabs who boast and seagulls proud.
They spin the yarns of sandy land,
With giggles shared 'neath the beach's band.

So let the ocean's laughter rise,
In funny waves and sunny skies.
Each ripple sways a tale untold,
A crazy wonder, bright and bold.

Whirlpools of Time and Space

In whirlpools where giggles spin,
A starfish claimed he'd just begun.
He spun so fast, lost his grip,
The ocean's whirl, a dizzy trip.

Mermaids on break from their throne,
Told stories of waves, then groaned.
With trident tricks and silly bets,
Laughter erupted in watery sets.

The tides conspired to shift the beat,
As sea creatures danced on their little feet.
You'd spot a shrimp doing the twist,
In this swirling oceanic mist.

So let the currents plot and twirl,
In the dance of the sea, life's a whirl!
With funny moments in every tide,
In this watery world, let joy abide.

Chasing the Horizon's Edge

I chased a fish, oh what a sight,
It wore a hat, a pure delight.
It winked at me, then took a dive,
I must admit, it's quite alive.

With seaweed jokes and jellybean glee,
The ocean laughed, just wait and see.
We danced on waves, too close I got,
A seagull swooped, said, 'Whoa, you rot!'

The sand tickled my sandy toes,
With crabby crickets playing shows.
The sun threw tantrums, painted skies,
While laughter echoed, oh, such highs!

In dreams of surf and salty air,
I found a fish who styled his hair.
His gills were wise, his scales were neat,
Together we pulled off quite the feat!

Murmurs of the Deep Blue

The octopus wore mismatched socks,
With eight left feet, he danced like rocks.
He tripped on coral, made a splash,
In the deep blue sea, in quite a flash.

The dolphins laughed, a bubbly crew,
With bubble gum and a wild zoo.
They played a tune, a surfy beat,
'Til sea turtles joined, oh what a feat!

Narwhals sang with flair and style,
Their unicorn horns made all of us smile.
They wiggled their tails, took us for rides,
While we forgot all our human prides.

A treasure chest held nothing but cheese,
"Come try it," said the fish with ease.
And there we feasted, oh, what a dream,
In the quirky waves, we made a team!

Beneath a Canopy of Stars

Under stars that twinkled bright,
The moon wore shades, oh what a sight!
Crabs threw parties in the sand,
They danced around, a merry band.

A starfish played the maracas loud,
While seashells gathered, oh they were proud.
The waves clapped hands, a joyful sound,
In underwater night, laughter was found.

The jellyfish glowed, disco lights galore,
We grooved along till we couldn't anymore.
The ocean's floor held secrets deep,
In dreams of fun, beauty did seep.

With laughter echoing far and wide,
The ocean's spirit was our guide.
In the night so bright, we lost all care,
Dancing beneath a glittering stare!

Secrets of the Briny Abyss

In the briny deep, secrets unfold,
Anemones gossip, their stories bold.
A clam wore glasses, spoke with pride,
"I've seen things, far and wide!"

The deep sea fish told silly tales,
Of singing whales and fish with scales.
They giggled at humans, always in sight,
"Why jump in water? It's a fright!"

An underwater mime tickled the shrimp,
Who went on strike, said, "You're such a wimp!"
The grouper chuckled, flipped his tail,
"Oh, to be human, that seems to fail!"

Yet amidst these laughs and silly tricks,
The ocean's pulse was all it depicts.
With laughter and joy, it spun around,
In the briny depths where fun is found!

The Coral Kingdom's Song

Underwater laughter bubbles bright,
Fish in bow ties dance, what a sight!
Jellyfish waltz, a slippery pair,
Crabs tap their claws with stylish flair.

Octopus chefs serve seaweed stew,
Conch shells play tunes, so funny and true!
Turtles in shades glide with delight,
While seahorses spin in the moonlight.

Starfish hold parties, they never quit,
With plankton cocktails, they sure make a hit!
The coral reef chuckles, colorfully grand,
In the kingdom where giggles rule the land.

Salt-kissed Memories

Seagulls squawk tales of olden days,
Of fishy pranks in sunlight's rays.
Sand castles tumble, kids in a roar,
As crabs pretend to be kings on the shore.

Kites soar high, tangled in glee,
While dolphins giggle, oh, can't you see?
Sandy toes wiggle, chasing the breeze,
Life's a beach party, so fun and at ease.

Barrels of laughter spill on the sand,
With shells as microphones, a rock band!
Every salt-kissed memory's packed with cheer,
As waves whisper secrets for all to hear.

A Siren's Gentle Call

From rocks she sings, a silly tune,
Bubbles bouncing under the moon.
Fish in bow ties dance with glee,
As the tide sways in harmony.

"Come hither!" she calls with a laugh so sweet,
While fish in tuxedos tap their feet.
But watch your step, oh sailor dear,
For slippery seaweed's always near!

Her voice, a giggle on ocean air,
Makes even the grumpiest whale stop and stare.
With every note, the sea comes alive,
Where silliness and laughter thrive.

Footprints in Luminous Sand

Barefoot dancers twirl on the shore,
Leaving footprints with stories galore.
Each step a whisper, a silly dance,
Caught in the tide—what a merry chance!

Tiptoeing crabs wave their claws,
Wiggling their bottoms without a pause.
Sunset giggles paint the sky,
As waves play tag and the stars wink by.

The sands sparkle, like laughter's trail,
Echoes of joy in each gusty gale.
Under the moon, the fun never ends,
In this magical spot where nature transcends.

Timeless Tides

In the wet socks of a sailor's plight,
Fishy tales twinkle through the night.
Waves that giggle, tides that play,
Each splash a laugh in the ocean's fray.

Seagulls gossip, always in flight,
Trading rumors of a fishy bite.
Dancing crabs on the sandy floor,
Who knew shells could hold such lore?

Salted breezes, a constant tease,
Coconut drinks with a hint of cheese.
Mariners chuckle at the sea's whim,
As they belly flop into a briny dim.

And so they sail, in hats that spin,
With tales of treasure they'll never win.
Though the sea may toss them about,
Their laughter rings, that's what it's about.

Fluid Fantasies

The lighthouse winked like a cheeky sprite,
While dolphins danced in the pale moonlight.
Each wave a giggle, each splash a sigh,
Who knew the ocean could be so sly?

Sandcastles crumble like dreams gone astray,
As tourists complain when the seas try to play.
A crab dons a hat, looks quite the sight,
While gulls steal chips, oh what a bite!

Mermaids chuckle with their hair like seaweed,
As sailors all grumble, downing their heed.
"Why can't we swim?" one sailor did pout,
"Because the fish are laughing, that's why we're out!"

But the ocean's charm can't be contained,
A hilarious chaos that can't be feigned.
With each tidal wave and salty spray,
They'll dive right in, it's a fun-filled day!

The Call of the Abyss

Down in the depths where the seaweed waves,
A fish wearing glasses misbehaves.
He flips through bubbles like a magazine,
As crabs tap dance, oh what a scene!

"Is that a shipwreck or a buffet treat?"
Beluga whales claim their mystical seat.
Octopus arms wave like they're on parade,
"Who's bringing the snacks?" they all serenade.

The anchor's tangled with gossip galore,
A seashell whispers as it opens its door.
"Bring some salsa and chips," it suggests,
For underwater parties, they're truly the best!

And while fish fight over the last little fry,
The laughter of sea life floats way up high.
For in the abyss, fun never abates,
It's just a big splash of barnacled mates!

Mariner's Twilight

As the sun dips low, the boat takes a spin,
Fishermen chuckle, let the wild tales begin.
"Did you see that wave? It nearly got me!"
"Oh, that's just the sea's own comedy!"

With nets full of jokes and stories galore,
The ocean's heart is a cabaret shore.
Mermaids giggle, causing a scene,
While sailors tease, "What's a fish in between?"

Is it dinner, or just a fishy tease?
A whale's belly laugh brings the boat to its knees.
The stars above twinkle, a whimsical sight,
While the mariners toast to the hilarity bright.

At the end of the day, the tides twist and churn,
Echoing laughter, for which they all yearn.
So they sail on, hearts light, full of glee,
For there's never a dull moment out at sea!

Footprints in the Sand

I walked along the sandy shore,
My footprints vanished, oh, what a chore!
A crab pinched my toe, what a surprise,
I danced away, much to its surprise.

I met a seagull, bold and brash,
It stole my sandwich, oh what a clash!
I chased it down, but to my dread,
It dropped my lunch, and snickered instead.

The sun was shining, oh so bright,
But sunscreen mixed up with my bite.
Sandy cheeks, a toddler made,
Giggled as I stumbled, unafraid.

As waves would crash with cheer and thrill,
I'd slip and slide, trip, and spill.
Yet here I laugh, I can't complain,
For footprints washed, I'll start again.

Echoes of the Seabreeze

The wind whistled tunes, oh so sly,
It played with my hat and made it fly.
A seagull laughed, perched on a post,
I pinched my nose, thought it a ghost.

A beach ball bounced with quite a flair,
It hit a fisherman, caught unaware.
His fishing rod flew high in the air,
Landed in a cooler, he couldn't bear!

Shells all around, I gathered a few,
One let out a sound, 'Who are you?'
I laughed out loud, oh what a show,
A funny little shell, with tales to know.

The breeze frolicked, dancing with glee,
Mischief maker, wild and free.
I waved goodbye to the salty tide,
In this silly moment, I took pride.

Meditations by the Shore

I sat on a rock, tried to find peace,
But a crab scuttled by, my thoughts would cease.
I pondered life, as waves crashed near,
And then slipped on slime, oh dear, oh dear!

My friend brought snacks, a picnic feast,
But ants joined in, the unwelcome beast.
They marched right up, in lines so neat,
I waved my hands, beat a hasty retreat.

A hermit crab peeked from its shell,
It looked at me, as if to yell.
'Why meditate when we can run?'
I chuckled aloud, so much for fun!

With seaweed wrapped like a fancy dress,
I laughed at my state, what a messy stress.
Meditations fail, but mood takes flight,
In laughter we find our own delight.

Chasing the Horizon

I spotted a fin, thought it was a shark,
But it was just a dolphin, making a spark.
He leapt and twisted, with such a style,
I tried to join in, fell down the aisle.

Chasing the sun, oh what a feat,
I raced the waves, my shoes on my feet.
But sand stuck fast, a sticky mess,
I slipped and laughed—a sandy dress!

With each step forward, the sun set low,
I danced with shadows, put on a show.
The horizon beckoned, a cheeky tease,
I tripped on a shell and dropped to my knees.

Yet here I stand, toes in the sand,
Giggling at life, isn't it grand?
With waves as my witness, I chase, I dream,
In this funny adventure, I find the theme.

Beneath the Waves

Fish in bow ties having a ball,
Bubbles popping like champagne, it's a fishy hall.
Octopus DJ spins records with flair,
Crabs do the conga without a care.

Seahorses prance in a regatta parade,
Jellyfish glow like lanterns displayed.
Starfish are judges, they clap their arms,
Coral reefs dance with quirky charms.

Celestial Currents

Turtles in space suits float by with grace,
Dolphins play tag in a zero-grav place.
Asteroids made of seaweed and sand,
Galactic parrotfish playing in a band.

Shooting stars drop pearls from the skies,
Mermaids giggle as they surf on the highs.
Cosmic waves rock boats of rainbow hues,
All night long, the ocean laughs and stews.

Echoes of the Deep

Whales tell jokes with a booming deep tone,
Their puns make fish giggle and groan.
In a hidden cave, a clam spills the tea,
Shells gossip wildly, just wait and see.

Crabs conduct symphonies, no one wants to miss,
With sea cucumbers swinging to bliss.
A conch shell croons tunes of laughter and fun,
Every scale and fin sizzles like sun.

Serene Shores

Seagulls wear shades, sipping tea on the sand,
While turtles write novels with a slow, steady hand.
Sandcastles tower, ambitious and bold,
While kids chase crabs, stories of old.

Laughter erupts like waves on the beach,
Where jellybeans float, just out of reach.
Seashells sharing secrets, a total delight,
Even the sun grins at this joyful sight.

A Constellation of Shells and Stars

On the shore, shells giggle aloud,
Whispers of tales from the ocean crowd.
A crab in a tux, what a sight to see,
Twirling in dance with a brave little flea.

A starfish plays cards with a wayward fish,
Plotting their heist for a jelly treat dish.
The waves roll in, with a foamy jest,
While seagulls debate which shell is the best.

Driftwood sings songs of old mariners past,
Dreams all tangled, but never outclassed.
A crab loses laughter, he's stuck in the sand,
While the seaweed does splits, oh isn't it grand?

So if you find laughter beneath the sea's gleam,
Join in the chaos, fulfill your wild dream.
For on this shore, with stars on display,
The ocean's a jester, come laugh, come play.

Serenade of the Seafarer's Dusk

As twilight descends, the gulls start to croon,
A mermaid sings softly, under the moon.
Her voice drips like honey, oh so absurd,
While dolphins dance wildly, not caring, not heard.

A pirate's out searching for treasure, they say,
But all that he finds is a crusty old tray.
He grumbles and gripes 'til a starfish does tease,
'The loot of the deep is like catching the breeze!'

The lighthouse is spinning, it's quite the ballet,
With beams of light tangled in a bright cabaret.
Crabs clap their claws for the seafarer's fun,
As fish put on hats, playing peekaboo sun.

So toast to the jesters, both fishy and bold,
For the tales they tell never quite get old.
A sunset soirée, where the sea laughs with glee,
And whimsy is king in this watery spree.

Ocean Whispers

At the beach, the seashells confide to the sand,
Crabs love to wiggle, they shimmy and stand.
A starfish enacts a grand slapstick show,
While waves keep on giggling, "Come on, don't be slow!"

Little sandpipers race in and out,
In chase of a shadow, they zoom all about.
They stumble and tumble, what a funny sight,
A comedy show as day turns to night.

The moonlight reflects on a slick oily eel,
Who dreams he's a dolphin, oh, what a big deal!
The fish roll in laughter, the seaweed joins in,
In this bubbling circus, we chase out the din.

So next time you wander by tides that do tease,
Remember the giggles that dance in the breeze.
For the ocean's a jester, so funny and free,
Where laughter and waves share the spirit of glee.

Tides of Memory

With each wave that laps, memories arise,
A clam wears a hat, oh, what a surprise!
He tells golden tales of the shipwrecked crew,
While starfish applaud, in a spectacle view.

The sun sets aflame, with hues bright and bold,
As fish dress in colors, all sparkly gold.
They gather round, sharing jokes from the deep,
While crabs crack up, in a loveable heap.

The seashells spin yarns about days gone by,
When snails rode the waves and learned how to fly.
A seahorse sneezes, creating a splash,
For the sea's full of whimsy, it's quite the bash!

So let's raise a glass to the tides we adore,
To the laughter and joy that keep coming ashore.
In the depths of the blue, where the happy fish swim,
Life's a funny affair, and oh, isn't it grim?

The Freedom of Ocean Air

Waves are dancing, birds in flight,
A seagull stole my sandwich, what a sight!
I'm sailing free with laughter loud,
The ocean air, it's like a cloud.

The boat tips over, splash goes me,
Fish are giggling, oh what glee!
I shout, 'Hey fish, let's have a race!'
They swim away, quick as a pace.

Sunsets paint the sky like art,
But I just tripped, oh dear, my heart!
The ocean laughs, it must know well,
My clumsy ways, my tales to tell.

With salty hair and glasses askew,
I'm a captain of fun, that's nothing new.
The ocean's breeze brings joy, it seems,
Life's a blast, filled with dreams!

Sailor's Heart

With a flip-flop on my left foot tight,
I chase the horizon, what a sight!
The waves are waves, they tickle my soul,
My sailor's heart is on a roll.

To the fish I sing my funny tune,
They wink and dance beneath the moon.
My compass spins in a silly way,
Leading me to the next buffet.

Anchors aweigh, but where's my hat?
Stolen again by a pesky cat.
I laugh at clouds, they puff like cream,
It's a whimsical, splashy dream!

In a boat of joy, we bob and weave,
Telling tales you won't believe.
With every wave, my heart does flip,
This is my fun nautical trip!

Wanderer's Path

Sailing down this wobbly track,
I met a crab with a sailor's knack.
He waved his claws and told a joke,
I laughed so hard, I nearly choked!

The map is upside down, oh dear,
But I'm still here, and full of cheer.
In a bottle, I found a note,
"Lost your way? Just float and gloat!"

A dolphin giggles, jumps so high,
It flipped and said, "Just give it a try!"
Through bubbles of laughter, we glide along,
A wanderer's life, a hum of song.

With every wave that sweeps the shore,
I find new friends, who could ask for more?
The ocean's whims, a funny delight,
In this seaside world, everything feels right!

Mysteries of the Moonlit Waters

Under the moon, the water shimmers bright,
A fish wears a tie, what a funny sight!
It glides on by, all dressed for a ball,
While I'm just trying not to fall.

The stars join in, they twinkle and wink,
Saying, "Hey, sailor, have a drink!"
I raise my cup full of salty cheer,
The moon laughs back, it's loud and clear.

Jellyfish dance in the silver glow,
And tell me secrets only they know.
They giggle softly, float and swirl,
I can't help but dance, give a twirl.

With each wave's tickle, a bubble does pop,
Moonlit mysteries make my heart stop.
The ocean's a stage, in this midnight play,
Where laughter reigns, come join the fray!

Nautical Dreams and Celestial Schemes

In a boat made of dreams, I set afloat,
The stars guide me, I'm the captain's note.
Gulls circle high, they squawk a tune,
Singing to the rhythm of the moon.

With a splash and a dash, I sail on through,
The fish are my friends, they love the view.
I tell them jokes, they bubble with glee,
In the watery world, we're fancy and free.

Navigating tides and silly schemes,
We chase the sunrise, and dance with beams.
The ocean's a playground, the sky's a stage,
In this whimsical life, we all engage.

So let's hoist the sails, let's make some noise,
With waves and laughter, we'll all rejoice.
From nautical dreams to celestial beams,
Life's a funny tale, or so it seems!

www.ingramcontent.com/pod-product-compliance
Lightning Source LLC
Chambersburg PA
CBHW072218070526
44585CB00015B/1391